DANIEL KEENE's plays have been produced widely throughout Australia and he is one of Australia's most internationally performed playwrights. During the thirty years in which he has written for the theatre, his plays have earned critical praise and sell-out seasons in theatres and at festivals in Australia, China, the United States and across Europe, especially in France, where more than eighty productions of his plays have been presented since 2000. His plays, which include *All Souls, Half and Half, The Serpent's Teeth, Silent Partner, Low, Terminus, The Architect's Walk, The Ninth Moon* and *Life Without Me* have received numerous literary awards, including the NSW Premier's Prize for literature three times, and the Victorian Premier's Prize for Literature twice. His groundbreaking and critically acclaimed collaboration with director Ariette Taylor – the Keene/Taylor Theatre Project (1997–2002) – was a major event in Australian theatre culture.

MOTHER

NINE SCENES

Daniel Keene

CURRENCY PRESS
SYDNEY

CURRENCY PLAYS

First published in 2015
by Currency Press Pty Ltd,
PO Box 2287, Strawberry Hills, NSW, 2012, Australia
enquiries@currency.com.au
www.currency.com.au

Copyright: © Daniel Keene, 2015.

COPYING FOR EDUCATIONAL PURPOSES

The Australian *Copyright Act 1968* (Act) allows a maximum of one chapter or 10% of this book, whichever is the greater, to be copied by any educational institution for its educational purposes provided that that educational institution (or the body that administers it) has given a remuneration notice to Copyright Agency Limited (CAL) under the Act.
For details of the CAL licence for educational institutions contact CAL, Level 15/233 Castlereagh Street, Sydney, NSW, 2000; tel: within Australia 1800 066 844 toll free; outside Australia 61 2 9394 7600; fax: 61 2 9394 7601; email: info@copyright.com.au

COPYING FOR OTHER PURPOSES

Except as permitted under the Act, for example a fair dealing for the purposes of study, research, criticism or review, no part of this book may be reproduced, stored in a retrieval system, or transmitted in any form or by any means without prior written permission. All enquiries should be made to the publisher at the address above.

Any performance or public reading of *Mother* is forbidden unless a licence has been received from the author or the author's agent. The purchase of this book in no way gives the purchaser the right to perform the play in public, whether by means of a staged production or a reading. All applications for public performance should be addressed to the author, c/- Currency Press.

Cataloguing-in-publication data for this title is available from the National Library of Australia website: www.nla.gov.au

Typeset by Dean Nottle for Currency Press.
Cover design by Wall2Wall Creative.
Front cover shows Botticelli's *Madonna of the Sea*.

Currency Press acknowledges the Traditional Owners of the Country on which we live and work. We pay our respects to all Aboriginal and Torres Strait Islander Elders, past and present.

Contents

MOTHER

One	1
Two	6
Three	11
Four	18
Five	22
Six	29
Seven	33
Eight	39
Nine	44

All goes unanswered, love is unanswered, out of the dark
A tongue without speech, a hand without touch, a crude potter's thumb,
Grooves us a moment, the Esperanto of sense
Jabbers our language, all that we hold in common.
Yet wings make grubs articulate, cocoons are spun for shattering,
And though you keep your hand over my mouth,
I will keep on singing, dry cicada under the spring.

                                            Dorothy Hewett
                              from *Unanswered Love Letter*

Mother was first produced by If Theatre at the Gasworks Arts Park, Melbourne, on 5 June 2015, with the following cast:

    CHRISTIE   Noni Hazlehurst

Director, Matt Scholten
Set, Costume and Props Designer, Kat Chan
Lighting Designer, Tom Willis
Sound Designer, Darius Kedros
Stage and Tour Manager, Ainsley Kerr

CHARACTER

CHRISTIE

She is about sixty years old. Her hair is long and unkempt. She wears a ragged, floral patterned dress that reaches to the ground. Her feet are bare, almost black with dirt.

SETTING

Various locations on the outskirts of a large city.

ONE

CHRISTIE *picking through rubbish on a block of vacant ground*
Crows calling
Bruised sky
Rust and rot

yes
that night when Lenny come home he smelt the drink on my lips
he said what's that
he knew what that was
how many times do I have to tell you he said
he'd told me a hundred thousand times
I don't know I said how many times
you promised you wouldn't he said
I know I did I said
what good's your promises he said you addled bitch
I'm not addled I said I'm as good as gold
funny he said you're funny
I'm not trying to be I said
I was often funny when I wasn't trying to be as far as Lenny was concerned
you don't know what's funny and what's not he said
I know more than you think I know I said
that's not much then he said you know next to nothing
next to nothing is not nothing I said it's something
and you don't know what it is I said
I don't want to know what it is he said
you do I said I can tell you want to know

no I don't he said I don't want to know nothing about you
then why'd you marry me I asked him
because I was lonely he said
I was lonely too I said
so that's what happened and we're not lonely anymore are we I said
he just looked at me with that look he'd get now and then
and I couldn't tell what he was thinking
but I knew it wasn't anything good
/
I took a drink because I needed a rest I explained to him
I needed a rest because of the baby who was very fractious today
very what he said
very fractious I said
what's that mean he said
the nurse at the clinic told me I said
she said I had a very fractious child
and do you know what it means he said
yes I said the nurse at the clinic explained it to me
explain it to me he said
I don't want to I said
because I'd forgotten what it meant exactly
except that there was a lot of crying involved
because the baby isn't comfortable in himself I said
what's wrong with him Lenny said
it's nothing serious I said he's got the gripe and he's not happy
a baby that little's not happy or sad he said he's too young
he doesn't know what he is
he doesn't have to know what he is I said

just because he doesn't know he's sad doesn't mean he's not sad

I thought he was fractious Lenny said

you don't even know what it means I said

neither do you he said

/

don't drink that stuff he said

where do you get it from he said

I'm not saying I said

then I didn't say anything else

and he just looked at me like I was a mad woman

/

it was from Mrs Kennedy that I got the drink

she lived two doors up the street

she was as old as a stone

she was kind to me when I needed a bit of relief

she was as mad as a budgie

but she knew how to mix a few things together

common stuff you could get anywhere

it was her mother's recipe from when times were worse she said

and I laughed when she said that

and so did she

when did it get easier she said

history doesn't happen to the poor

and then she laughed again

and I didn't know what she meant or what I should say

but she didn't seem to care

/

turpentine was in it I know that much

I always had it with a bit of powdered milk mixed in to help it down
she called it the good stuff
better than anything you could buy in the shops she said
and I gave her a little payment for it when I could
although she always said I didn't need to pay her
but I always did when I could afford to
/
Lenny sat down at the kitchen table and I gave him his dinner like a good wife is supposed to
and he ate it while I sat looking out the window
aren't you eating he said
I'm not hungry I said
have you fed the baby he said
of course I have I said
what did you feed him
I fed him mashed banana
is that all
that's all he needs
how do you know he said
because I'm his mother I said what would you feed him
of course he didn't know what he'd feed him
you know nothing about children I said
then Lenny didn't say nothing for a while
he just fiddled with the food on his plate
like a little boy who can't get his own way
which is what he was like when he couldn't think of what to say
which was very often the case
/
I can't sit here all night I said I've got things to do

no-one's asking you to sit here all night he said
what have you got to do you can hardly walk straight he said
have you washed the baby's clothes at least
yes I have I said he hasn't got many
they're out hanging on the line if you want to take a look
of course he couldn't take a look because it was dark by now
and there was no light out in the yard
when are you going to fix that light I said
he didn't answer me
he just stood up and scraped what was left on his plate into the bin
that's a waste I said all that food you're throwing out
it's not much he said
didn't you like it I said
no I didn't he said
so that was dinner over and done with
/
I woke up in the middle of the night and the bed was empty beside me
so I got up and went to the bedroom door
and I stood there listening
and I heard Lenny singing to the baby
and it was like the baby was singing back
gurgling and whispering with that tiny voice of his
and it sounded so far away
as if the baby being so young made him a long way from us
and there was his dad trying to sing him back
to sing him back home to us

TWO

CHRISTIE *on an empty street*
Footfalls
Stink of diesel
Rain

I've got nothing
I never had much but I've got nothing now
for some people that's as good as me being a criminal
I'm treated like a criminal
the looks I get are terrible
I have to turn away
I don't know what my face must look like
I hope that it doesn't look like I feel
I'd hate to think I looked like that
I don't want my feelings on show because I'm ashamed of them
I never thought I'd feel like I do when people look at me
I never thought I'd feel so worthless
I couldn't have imagined such a thing
I imagined different things about myself
I forget what they were
but they were better
I thought better of myself
I don't think anything about myself now
I've given all that up
I wouldn't know how to anymore
I don't know who I am

I'm just nobody
/
who knows what I might have been
or even who I was once upon a time
there's no what might have been and no what will be anymore
I wake up every day thinking it might be my last
and sometimes I lie down at night wishing it had been
/
a little boy chased me a few weeks ago
like a wild little bird he was
pecking at my heels and calling me all sorts of names
he couldn't have been more than ten years old
but the language he used would have shamed a fucking navvy
you get away from me I said you get back home where you belong
but he didn't take no notice
he just kept at me like a magpie peck peck pecking
so I had to turn around to him and lift my hand
I said to him if you don't leave me alone I'll give you a crack around the earhole
and then he laughed he cackled
you've got arseholes for earholes he said
haven't you got nothing better to do than cause me fucking trouble I said
no he said I fucking haven't
so I took a swing at him and caught him right across the top of the head
and his head was as hard as a rock
he just stood there looking at me
cunt he said you old cunt piss off out of my street you old cunt

it's not your street I said

anyone who wants can walk down this street and no-one's got a right to stop them

you stink he said

I might stink I said but I know my rights

and I've got manners too which is more than I can say for you

cunt he said sneering at me like a mad rat

so I leaned down close to him

I looked right into his screwed-up little face and I said listen

I said you go home and tell the cunt you came out of that she's got a cunt for a son and he didn't say nothing after that

so I just turned and went on my way as if I didn't have a care in the world

but my heart was racing and I could hardly walk

I felt so weak and I suppose I was afraid

not of that kid but of everything

I was suddenly afraid of everything in the world

/

so that's how I'm treated on a regular basis

but I've learned how to stick up for myself

which is something I only learned very late

the rest of my life I was never able to say a good word for myself

and was never able to stop those that wanted to hurt me from hurting me

there's some people who like nothing better than to come at you like a rabid dog

and there's nothing you can do to protect yourself

but you have to learn to take the slings with the arrows as they say

and look after yourself as best you can

no matter how bruised and battered you might feel
which in my case is most of the time
/
I've not seen that little rat-face again
I think I must have put the wind right up him
I've walked down that street of his other times and he hasn't shown his face
he had a sweet face really when it wasn't screwed up with hatred
that's what it was it was hatred
it's a hard thing to see it in someone so young
but it's not a surprise to me anymore
I've seen it more than once
I can't account for it
I suppose there's all kinds of reasons someone so young can be so sour inside
I wonder if my little boy would have turned out the same
but I find it hard to think that he would have
he would have been kind I'm sure of it
all he knew was kindness
but maybe that don't matter
maybe he would have forgotten all of that
when he got out into the world and had his heart broken
most likely he would have been too weak to defend himself against all the cruelties he would have found
but he was spared all that
he was spared it like I haven't been
I'm the one who's got hard
and he's stayed as soft as he was
which is a kind of blessing

for him I mean
a blessing for him
/
it's not a blessing for me

THREE

CHRISTIE *in a rest home armchair*
Dust
Stillness
Last words ill-heard

they let me in here when I'm too down in the dumps to stay outside
outside is where I'm happiest
but even the happiest times can turn miserable
that's as easy done as said
sometimes it happens so quick that I think to myself I'm living in a dream
you're dreaming Christie I say to myself
you were always dreaming that's the truth I know it is
I'm not afraid of the truth
I never have been
I may have avoided it now and then
but it wasn't being afraid of it that made me
not afraid for myself anyway
it was always other people who couldn't be told
who mustn't be told
you tell some people the truth and they can't take it in
it ruins them
I've seen it
/
I had to tell my father he was dying
my mother couldn't do it I can't do it

Christie I can't do it she said slobbering like an old dog
so I had to
the doctor said it might be best coming from one of the family
and I was all the family there was
/
my father was in some shithole of a place where they put the terminal
the poor ones anyway
but he didn't catch on
he was a bit gone in the head by then
his liver was gone completely
but he liked to think that he'd battle on
he always thought that he could battle on
I think that being pissed most of the time helped him think so
but I had to walk in there and tell him he was on his way out
so I got led into the public ward by the nurse
who drew the screens around us as quiet as you like
then she was off
I thought there was no use beating around the bush
so I just come out with it as plain as I could make it
you're dying Dad I said they told me that you're dying
he didn't speak
he just stared at me like he didn't know who I was
then he shut his eyes
that was the last I saw of him
he was dead that night
I've often wondered what would have happened if I'd told him he was doing good
and that there was nothing to worry about

he might have hung on a bit longer
although I don't know what for seeing the state he was in
it would make the cat weep
he was as yellow as old wallpaper and weak as a baby
it was me telling him that killed him
it was knowing he was dying that was the cause of death
/
I know that I'll be dead one day as well
but I'm not going to let knowing that kill me
/
there are mad old women in here all dying from one thing or another
some of them are going quietly they hardly wrinkle the sheets
there's others who don't stop moaning day and night
oh I'm in pain they say in terrible pain
well pain's all relative isn't it love
we're all in fucking pain one way or another I tell them
I've got no time for pain
I've got no interest in it
how can I be interested in something as common or garden as pain
it'd be like being interested in breathing
/
they call this place a rest home
it's a laugh isn't it
the next stop's the morgue and everyone knows it
there's a room out the back where they put the corpses before they're carted off they've offered me a bed but I said no
you might as well put me straight into a coffin as into a bed in this place

I've got no intention of dying just at the moment I tell them
it's all charity in here of course
it's all about the good deeds of the few to ease the suffering of the many
there's a lot of that goes on
I don't know what good it does anyone
I saw an old girl sitting in a bus stop not long ago
dead as a doornail she was
her little bit of shopping on the bench beside her
she didn't know what hit her probably
but there she was doing what she always did when she dropped off the twig
not stuck in a bed among strangers all waiting for the end
it's like walking the fucking plank as far as I'm concerned
/
I used to have the baby in bed with me when he was very new
he was like a little hot water bottle
Lenny didn't like it much
I can't get to you he said
get to me for what I said
you know what he said
well I'm not interested in that right at the moment I said
when will you be he said
I don't know I said I've got other things on my mind
what things he said
I'm a new mother now I said and my life's changed
I've got to sort myself out
sort what out he said
how do I know I said I'm just getting started

what am I supposed to do in the meantime he said
you have to be patient I said
he didn't like that too much
but I wasn't budging
and I put my arms around the baby and lifted him up and laid him on my belly
we haven't thought of a name yet I said
what should we call him
call him anything you like said Lenny
you have to like the name too I said
he didn't say nothing
/
I think Lenny didn't know the baby very well
so he didn't know what to call him
but he knew how to love him
/
yes he loved him I know that
/
something from the Bible I said that's always good
a name that means something and that you can read stories about
how about Jacob I said
Lenny said that sounds like a Jewish name
and I said it was a Jewish name
and Lenny said we're not Jewish
we're not anything I said
but Lenny didn't want a Jewish name
why don't you want him to have a Jewish name I said
Lenny didn't answer he just shrugged

what about Abraham I said just to have a laugh
for fuck's sake Lenny said
Irish names were out too
and so were any of the names of the royal family who were just scum the lot of them according to Lenny
there aren't many names left I said
what about Lenny he said
but that's your name I said
it can be his name too he said
I wouldn't know who was who I said
yes you would he said
and I knew I would I suppose
but I wasn't sure the baby wanted to be called Lenny
he wants his own name I said
it would be his name Lenny said
but it's your name as well I said
what's wrong with my name he said
there's nothing wrong with your name I said
I think it's a beautiful name it's a beautiful name because it suits you
how does it suit me he said
it just does because that's who you are I said
you're Lenny
what would you rather be called I said
you could have your name changed if you wanted
I don't want my bloody name changed he said
if you changed your name then we could call the baby Lenny and there wouldn't be any mix-ups
what would I be called he said

MOTHER

I don't know I said
how about Adam
and I could change my name to Eve
you're a bloody idiot he said
/
so we called the baby Lenny and Lenny stayed Lenny as well

FOUR

CHRISTIE *in a church*
Cold light
Brief echoes
Smell of priest

when I was left alone with the baby I called him something else
I called him Beau
because I read somewhere that Beau means beautiful
I never told Lenny
/
those were lovely times alone with Beau
I'd make a nest with the bedclothes
and we'd lie in there in the afternoon all dozy
and I'd make little cooing and whistling sounds
and pretend that we were all alone in the world
all alone in the big tree I imagined we were in
I imagined the sky and the sunshine on our wings and the grubs I'd feed Beau
and I'd peck at him with my fingers peck peck
I'd hold him high in the air over my head
and he'd look down at me and he was flying
and he wasn't afraid
he was a bird as much as the bird just outside the window or in the tree in the front yard or in the sky over the house
and I'd forget about the damp in the passage and the paint peeling in the kitchen

and the cupboards empty most days and the hole in my one pair of stockings
and the stink of the sewer from the drain out the back
and the drink I kept hidden in the laundry under the trough
I didn't need a drink or the sorrow and the tears that came with it
nor the ache in my guts after
and I'd forget Lenny in the kitchen doorway when he came home from work
his face black with the heaviness of the day
and me less than he wanted me to be
and him less than himself
/
they were beautiful days
/
I come in here to bless myself with the holy water
and to have a bit of a wash if no-one's watching
the water's so cold
you think they'd warm it when they pour it over a baby's head
but they don't
no wonder the poor little buggers cry when they're baptised
but I suppose that's another coming into the world
your head soaked in cold water
and someone jabbering at you about God and the devil
I don't believe in God and I'd be surprised if he believed in me
he'd be a cruel bastard if he did exist
still I like to bless myself now and then
it's got nothing to do with God
I like to be blessed by the water

being blessed means everything's not so bad for a moment
for a few seconds
it's just you and the cold water
/
I saw God in a dream once
he was an eye in a black cloud
the cloud was like a giant rock in the sky
and the eye was all milky white like a soft boiled egg
and he was looking looking looking
/
Lenny come home one night and the baby was crying
I was sitting at the kitchen table with my hair hanging down
and all the weight of the world on me where too much of the drink had put it
I couldn't answer
I couldn't hear the baby crying
I looked up at Lenny and I said he's alright I said he's been good today
and Lenny's off through the house down the dark passage narrow as a gutter
his big man's shoulders banging on the walls
his big boots thumping
he's off through the house like an animal down the chute
his rough hands swinging his eyes dark as a cold night
and into the front room where flies were buzzing
the baby's nappy full of shit
a crust of snot under his nose
belly-up on the carpet his arms flung out like he was waiting for the nails

he's good I said he's good I shouted from the kitchen chair

Christ there's me as well you know

in this coffin of a house you nail it shut every morning you go out the door

then Lenny come back into the kitchen holding the baby

liar I said liar

you said you loved me

I'm still here I said

don't you dare lay a hand on me

/

there were other nights I don't remember how many

the baby crying and Lenny as quiet as a stone standing in front of me

his face tired and pale and his tired hands around my hands

Christie he'd say Christie

and then he didn't know what to say

and I didn't know what he was asking or what he wanted

and I could feel the drink coming up in my throat

and the stink on my lips

and I wanted to howl but nothing would come out

nothing

/

then one night I woke up and the bed was empty beside me

and the baby was just a round hollow in the pillow where his head had been lying

FIVE

CHRISTIE *on a park bench*
Birds' wings
Shadows
Wet earth

my mother told me she told me so
the old hag gnawed her gums her breasts flat as plates under her cardigan
I told you she said I told you you'd never be a good mother
like you weren't I said
she slapped me with her flatiron of a hand and my nose bled
/
she was sitting in her rented room at the back of a cobbler's
the cobbler pounding nails the other side of the wall
the place stank of shoe polish and glue
and her rotting towards seventy
/
what did you come here for she said
I can't do anything I can't change anything
I don't want anything changed I said
I want everything like it was
she said nothing just stared at me
and she had cockroaches for eyes
I'm going mad I said
don't make me laugh she said
and the cockroaches were crawling down her cheeks

MOTHER

you were mad when you married that man
and the cockroaches were sitting on her lips
I told you he was no good she said
and the holes where her eyes had been had been stitched shut with black thread
don't look at me like that she said
and cockroaches swarmed in her mouth
I'm going mad I said
Mama please
and I reached out to pull the thread from her eyes
Mama please
but she couldn't hear me anymore
and I saw her shrink down in her chair to a lump of threads
like something the cat sicked up
Mama I said please
I'm going mad

/

Lenny sent me a note
I'm at my sister's are you straightened out yet it said
I was straight as a broom handle
I went round there in a clean dress and my hair combed
are you coming back I asked him
he looked at me hard his fists jammed down in his pockets
where's the baby I said
my sister's taking care of him he said
your fucking sister I said
and I could see his neck tighten
are you straight he said

so I breathed in his face
what do you smell I said
toothpaste he said
I'm allowed to brush my teeth I said
then I heard the baby crying
he wants me I said
he doesn't know you're here said Lenny
of course he does I said babies can tell if their mothers are close I said
they can smell them or something
if you don't smell of grog then how can he know it's you said Lenny
don't break my heart I said
haven't you got any feeling I said
he just stood there like a tombstone
and I suddenly come over all dizzy
and I fell
I fell right there on the front doorstep
and that bastard didn't even bend down to pick me up
/
I was still on my hands and knees when I saw Beau coming down the passage
he was on his hands and knees as well
as he come towards me
he must have thought I was playing
/
we had a lovely time until Lenny said I had to go and picked up the baby
I said I was taking the baby with me
and he said not on your life
I said the baby was my life

and Lenny just stood there with the baby in his arms and said pig's arse he is
that's when I started howling and couldn't stop
I could hear myself howling like an animal
it didn't sound like me
it was just a sound coming out of me
I didn't know where it was from
Lenny's face went white and he pulled the baby close
and he put out his arm and pushed me back out the front door
and I was left standing on the step when the door shut
/
I was still howling when the cops came
now missus they said what's all this
now missus they said
and one of them put his hand around my wrist
I could feel his wedding ring pressing into me right on the bone
so I took a swing at him and caught him on the side of his head
and his hat flew off
and then I was in the van
and I was carted off like a lump of fucking meat
/
the police know all kinds of people who say they want to help you
they can't help you
because they don't know what you need
you can't tell them what you need
you don't know what it is
it might be money
most of the time it would be money
but you can't ask for money

they haven't got any money to give you
and money's not the answer they say
not the answer to what
to whatever's bothering you
being poor's bothering you
but apparently money's not the answer
if it isn't I don't know what is
/
after that day I visited on Sunday afternoons
with Lenny leaning over me like a warden
I whispered Beau in the baby's ear so Lenny couldn't hear me
and the baby giggled
Lenny's sister was always there
she had a keyhole for a face
thin as a ferret and a churchgoer of course
as barren as a plank and just as hard
/
Lenny was like a little kid in front of her
I knew he loved me
I could see it in his eyes when he looked at me with the baby in my arms
but he couldn't let her see that look
I knew what she thought of me
he had to think it too when she was around
and she was always around
she stuck to Lenny like shit to a blanket
/
it was a stinking summer

MOTHER

the country dried out

cockatoos came into town from the hills

screeching over Brunswick and Collingwood

they sat on telephone poles and tram wires

gangs of them screaming like banshees

when they shook their feathers clouds of red dust came off them like smoke

they sat along the guttering of the Rising Sun Hotel

and on the chimneys of the Grace Darling in Smith Street

their beaks stuck open going mad with hunger

dust storms blew in and the sky went dark yellow

you'd have to shut your eyes and mouth

I put a scarf around my head like an Arab

and pushed against the wind down Johnston Street my dress flapping like a sail

I cadged drinks in the Prince Patrick and the Crown

and at the Leinster Arms in Gold Street

until they barred me for being a nuisance

and I had to stay outside with the cockies dying of thirst

/

I saw Mrs Kennedy most days

and she gave me some of her good stuff to get me through

because she knew how it was she said

you could see she'd had a rough time or two

there was something in her eyes that told you she'd seen the worst

she never said nothing about herself and I never asked

I just told her that I thought she was a good woman

I don't know what that is she said

but I know you've got to survive no matter what
and I don't know whether that makes you good or bad
/
I wanted to ask if she thought I was good or bad
but I didn't dare

SIX

CHRISTIE *inside a derelict house*
Cold rooms
Rats scratching
Stains

when Lenny stopped paying the rent on the house I went round to his sister's place to see him and he wouldn't even let me inside

so I stood there on the front step like a fucking beggar

and he told me that I could move in with him and his sister

there was a sleepout I could have

he wasn't paying for a place where he didn't live

and I said aren't you coming back

but he didn't answer

you'd be close to the baby was all he said

and so you and your sister can keep eye on me I said

I'm thinking about you and the baby he said

oh yeah I said

I might as well be a corpse as in that sleepout I said

what kind of life would I have living like that out the back

with eyes on me day and night

what kind of a life have you got now he said

my own life I said

I want what's best he said

best for who I said not for me I said

for the baby for the baby he said

pig's arse I said

he should be with me I said
he should be with his mother
Christie he said
Christie have you looked at yourself lately
every morning when I have a wash I said
I see myself staring back
I see that baby's mother
I see empty arms where a baby should be
I see hands with nothing to do
I see a mouth that hasn't been kissed
I'm dried out with crying I said
I'm heavy inside like someone's cut me open and stitched a lead
    weight inside me
like someone's taken a stick to me
look in my eyes Lenny
look in my eyes and tell me what you see
/
he didn't say nothing for a while
he wouldn't look at me
you can move into the sleepout any time you want he said
what if I don't want to I said
then I don't know what you'll do he said
and that was the end of it
he turned away shut the door
/
I went home and looked at myself
I wanted to see what Lenny had seen
something had made him turn away from me

MOTHER

but how can you turn away from yourself
you've got to see yourself when you're not looking
you've got to look at yourself as though you're someone else
how can you do that
/
I sat on the back step of the house that wasn't mine anymore
I sat there as night-time filled the backyard
all the green weeds and the flowers I'd planted
and the vegetables dying in the plots that Lenny had dug
were all disappearing into the dark
and I tried to see myself
to see what Lenny saw and what my mother saw
and what the baby saw
I saw my hands on Lenny's skin
and my hands holding the baby's tiny hands
and I saw my arms around my mother
helping her into bed and all her ruined life like sweat on her skin
and I saw my face against Lenny's face
on our pillows in our bed in our house that wasn't ours anymore
and I saw my baby's face still raw from being inside me pressed into
  my soft belly
and I saw my arms red from the hot water in the trough
and my hands wringing out the sheets and hanging them on the
  clothesline
I saw my face rounded on the side of an empty bottle
and staring at me from the window of the Rising Sun Hotel
I saw my face bruised by the back of my father's hand
and I saw my face kissed by Lenny

I saw my face in the black glass of the kitchen window when the
    night was late
and I was sat there my hands on my knees and my hair hanging down
and the baby crying in the front room
I saw my face the way I'd never seen it and the way I'd always seen it
and I looked out into the backyard
where the washing on the clothesline flapped like a bird against the
    cold of the sky
and that was all I saw
/
I don't remember the next days
just Mrs Kennedy feeding me the good stuff
me not much of myself just in pieces
and the looks of neighbours
like sharpened knives when I shut the house behind me
and left for good
/
I left the key in the door
I never went back
nobody lived there anymore

SEVEN

CHRISTIE *in a narrow lane*
Reek of piss
Junkies' leavings
Shine of puddles

the trains went by on the Upfield line behind Lenny's sister's house
I was welcome in the house at dinner time
and I could lay the baby down to sleep at night
I'd sing him a song but I knew he was forgetting who I was
they pushed him to church on Sundays
but I wouldn't go
Lenny's sister pushed the pram like the fucking baby was hers
I laughed
I said if it was hers it must have been an immaculate conception
/
the trains went by to Upfield and back
the mirror rattled on the wall when they passed
and my face in the mirror trembled
I went in and out as much as I liked
I used the back gate and down the sideway
I didn't go through the house
when I heard Beau crying in the night I put my ear against the window of the sleepout I heard Lenny singing to him from across the yard
/
all the houses were grey and all the people in the houses were grey

the whole world was like an old photograph that had been left in the sun
the edges of the world were curled up and brittle
I stopped wearing shoes
I thought if I wore shoes I'd tear a hole in the world and fall through
I don't know where I thought I'd end up
but I stepped as light as bird
I kept to the lanes
I knew all the lanes between Collingwood and Brunswick
some were like gardens and some like sewers
I'd hear kids playing in their backyards and dogs barking
and different languages and music playing
I'd smell hot dinners cooking and grass just mowed
I'd go along close to the fences and feel all the life on the other side
I'd go very early in the morning or late at night
when the whole world was like a river that had stopped running
and there was just me
moving as quiet as a bird
/
I got so lonely that I wasn't lonely anymore
that's what happens to people
when that happens they're gone
nothing in the world can bring them back
/
I think I was a child again
I let my hair go wild and spat in the street
my feet were scuffed and hard
and there were scabs on my knees where I'd fallen over outside the Railway Hotel

MOTHER

I played peekaboo with Beau and whispered his secret name
I stood outside the Cornish Arms and sang songs for drinks
and in the Moreland Hotel I could collect the empties
as long as I didn't bother anyone
and they'd give me a couple of bottles to bring home to the sleepout
clink clink up the sideway
Lenny's sister's eyes like two wormholes
looking out at me through the flowered curtains
/
I remember Lenny watching me from the kitchen window
his eyes pouring love all over me through the white blossom in the backyard floating down like snow
/
it was never about love
I loved Lenny and Lenny loved me
and we loved the baby
/
but something went black inside me
something burned and cracked like a bone left in the fire
something that seemed to weigh as much as the world
and all the love in the world couldn't shift it
nothing could fix it
I went to Mama and I told her about it
she looked at me the way you look at a beaten dog
Christie there's nothing you can do she said
I think it must be meant to be she said
there's some who have to carry the weight of the world
then she pulled out a string of rosary beads and held them in the cup of her hands

and she told me about Jesus who was just like me she said
he was just like all of us
the poor bugger suffered for us she said and we suffer for him
I had to laugh out loud
Jesus must be hard up if he needs you for a friend I said
God help us all if it's come to that
you little bitch she said
and she held the cross up in her fist and put it right up to my face
fuck off with that I said
you're nailed to your cross my girl she said
you're nailed to your cross like all of us
she almost screamed at me
and her fist was shaking and the cross was shaking in her fist
and she lifted herself out of her chair and stood bent over almost double
with her tits sagging inside her nightdress and her hair hanging down
and the tears pouring from her eyes
and she opened her mouth and wailed
and a long string of spit was hanging off her bottom lip
and then I knew she wasn't long for the world
I knew that she was dying
she was always dying
but she was dying properly now
she was as close to death as she was to me
me just stood there not knowing what to do
just howling Mama Mama crying too like she was
it would have been a sight if anyone had seen us
but there was no-one to see us

there was no-one but us two mother and daughter howling
and death right there in the room with us
and Jesus of course
nailed up on his little silver cross trembling in her fist
/
I never went back
/
I went home to the sleepout after I'd seen Mrs Kennedy
and I had more than a few just to give myself the strength I needed
that black bone was still heavy inside me
and cracking cracking
children run past me in the street and one of them spat at me
they was like little dogs yapping and biting
but I paid them no heed
the world swam all around me
it was like I was walking under water
but I got to the sleepout at last through the gate and up the sideway
I heard Beau crying inside the house as I passed but I paid no heed
there was nothing I could do for him nothing I could mend nothing I could change
I curled up on my bed I stayed there for I don't know how long
until I looked up and I saw Lenny standing over me
and he was saying it was time to go
time to go where I said
and he didn't say nothing
he just lifted me up off the bed like I was a child and set my two feet on the floor
and walked me to the door and up the sideway to the front gate

it was dark by then and there was a man standing out on the footpath waiting

he put out his hand and I took hold of it

but I couldn't seem to grip nothing

and I said time to go where

then I can't remember nothing else

except I was on my knees in some room I didn't know

and I was throwing up into a plastic bucket

my hair was all hanging down in the sick and I stank

I stank

/

I came to in the ward

I was in a bed with clean white sheets and the curtain drawn around me

and I was crying

I don't know why

and it was like the first time I'd ever cried in my life

EIGHT

CHRISTIE *on vacant ground*
Black hollows
Sewer stink
Rustle of weeds

Mama died while I was in the madhouse
someone found her in her room on the floor beside her bed
and there was ants crawling on her
she must have been there a while
Lenny saw to it she had a decent burial
which meant the hole was deep enough and there was something to mark the spot she's with her Jesus now
I hope he appreciates the effort she made to believe in him
/
I tried to pray to Jesus once or twice
but I was just talking to myself
that's how you drive yourself mad I said
is it I said
yes it is I said
then I won't pray no more I said
good for you I said
and that was the end of it
/
of course they don't call it a madhouse
they called it a hospital
but I was still locked up

way back when even if you was mad they never locked you up
you were allowed to wander about
you were a sort of amusement
I suppose that's what I am now to some people
but I'm not mad
I've thought I was once or twice
but I've always been lucky enough to come across someone worse off than me
there's a great comfort in that
it's a real pick-me-up when you come across some poor bastard worse off than yourself
but they're few and far between as far as I'm concerned
of course you can still find them
living in a drain or under a fucking rock somewhere
no I've never been mad
but I've had terrible storms in my head
great claps of thunder and rain inside my head
like in one of them glass things you shake to make it snow
and sheets of lightning going on and off inside my head
like giant light bulbs exploding
it still happens now and then
/
as soon as I got out I went to see Mama
fucking pointless really
but I felt I had to
I stood beside the trampled-down piece of dirt and I thought how small it was
that's all I thought
/

Mama I said as if she could hear me
Mama I said I'm a better mother than you were
I hope that before I die my baby will know I love him
which is more than I ever knew about you
and that's a shame I said
but there's nothing can be done about that
like a lot of things that nothing can be done about
Jesus or no Jesus
/
I walked around the graveyard thinking this is where I'll be one day
it's a relief to know there's a place where no-one can bother you
except those that were supposed to have loved you
/
Lenny had stopped locking the back door since I'd been away
I come in the house through the back door
and I walked down the passage to the baby's room and I stood in the doorway
/
I stood in the doorway and I reached for the light switch in the dark
/
I reached for the light switch in the dark and the light come on and I saw him
/
I was still wearing the little paper wristband they give you in the madhouse
with your name written on it
which is I suppose in case you forget
I looked at it and I said my name out loud

Christie

/

he was lying there as bright as day
his eyes wide open
and he was looking at me
and I knew he didn't know who I was anymore

/

you're mine I said
and I moved closer to him
the house was quiet Lenny and his sister were asleep in their rooms down the passage and I thought of Lenny alone in his bed
and I wondered did he still reach out for me in the night like he used to
even when he was asleep
and even though I was asleep I'd feel him reaching
and I'd turn to be closer to him
and how quiet it was when our bodies touched
how marvellous it was that bodies touching made no sound at all
and I wondered did he still lie with his body curved to the shape of mine
even though I wasn't there

/

I leaned down to Beau and I said have you been lying awake in the dark

/

I'm Christie I said I'm your mum

/

I climbed in bed with him and he let out a little cry
it was a sound so small but it tore right through me

MOTHER

maybe only a mother can hear that sound
or maybe only love knows that sound
only love can sound like that
love when it's forgotten or love when it's found
or love like a hungry bird squawking
he was my hungry little bird
and I pecked him with my fingers like I used to to make him laugh
but he didn't laugh
there were tears falling from his eyes like little stones
and then I thought I heard Lenny's boots coming down the passage
his shoulders knocking on the walls either side
how many times have I told you Christie
his sister right behind him with her Bible voice and her eyes out on stalks
I squeezed Beau close to me
I wanted him to be quiet
I wanted him to be like he was when he was inside me
I wanted him to be as quiet as that
and not know how cruel the world can be
why should he know that
/
but no-one came down the passage
not Lenny or his sister or no-one
it was just me and Beau and with the light still turned on
and I fell asleep with Beau wrapped in my arms
/
he didn't make a sound the whole night
he didn't move

NINE

CHRISTIE *with a bunch of wildflowers*
Frost
Trembling hands
Stars

he only ever had one candle
one candle shaking when he breathed on it
I saw how his eyes opened wide
I could see the candle shaking in his eyes
/
do you know what you've done they said
/
I reached for the light switch in the dark I said
I saw him lying there with his eyes wide open
he'd been lying in the dark like that for God knows how long
he didn't know who I was I said
/
he wasn't here long
not long enough to speak
if only I could have heard him speak
all the words are lost
all I never got to have and all I never gave him
what would I give him
not tears not curses
I'd light two candles for him then three and every year one more
until we could switch off the light and still see our faces
his and mine with another year between us

and no time wasted falling down drunk
and me a good mother and him a good son
/
yes that night when Lenny come home he smelt the drink on my lips
he said what's that he knew what that was
how many times do I have to tell you he said
it wasn't the first time or the last
there weren't any last times then
/
I stood in the doorway and I saw him looking at me
and I wondered how long he had been lying in the dark like that
waiting for me to come to him
/
lost I've lost all of him pale hair and a first tooth and lost all of me
/
I thought I saw him walking down the passage and out the front door
I thought I saw him standing on the roof of the sleepout
I thought I saw him hiding under the table in the kitchen
I saw him walking with my mother near her grave
I saw him with a bottle of stout in the Railway Hotel
I saw him in the madhouse weeping
I saw him carrying Lenny crying in his arms
I saw him asleep in the bed beside me
a grown man wearing boots and overalls
with a shovel in his hand
he was my gravedigger lying there beside me
his eyes wide open
they were eyes of polished stone
lost lost lost he's lost what is he now

dead skin dead bones
never happy never sad never old
a voice I won't hear
a face I won't touch
an empty bowl and empty spoon
a withered leaf I can crumple in my hand
or press here on my breast and feel it break
/
I know what I've done I said
don't tell me what I've done
I said I'll grow old and go barefoot
all mothers grow old and walk on stones
I'll have no face and no name anyone remembers
he would have remembered me
he would have been the last to remember
maybe in a dark room somewhere
a grown man lying awake thinking of me before he fell asleep
he would have felt my hand on his face again
have you been lying awake in the dark I'd say
have you been waiting for me to come to you
/
I'm here I'd say
I'm here

Frost
Trembling hands
Stars

THE END

www.ingramcontent.com/pod-product-compliance
Lightning Source LLC
Chambersburg PA
CBHW050027090426
42734CB00021B/3450